March of America Facsimile Series

Number 1

Epistola de Insulis Nuper Inventis

Cristoforo Colombo

Epistola de Insulis Nuper Inventis

by Cristoforo Colombo

with an English Translation
by Frank E. Robbins

ANN ARBOR
UNIVERSITY MICROFILMS, INC.
A Subsidiary of Xerox Corporation

Foreword

The Columbus Letter of 1493 is the first printed account of the New World. In it Christopher Columbus reports what he has experienced during his first voyage. Originally written in Spanish, the letter was translated into Latin by a Catalan named Leander di Cosco and spread the news of Columbus' discovery all over Europe.

Columbus composed his famous letter aboard the "Niña," the ship on which he made the homeward passage after the flagship "Santa Maria" was wrecked off Haiti. Columbus suspected—with good reason—that Martin Alonso Pinzón, captain of the "Pinta," the third caravel taking part in the voyage, might try to beat him to Ferdinand and Isabella with the good news and reap all the glory of the discovery. The date of the Spanish letter, February 15, seems to indicate that Columbus meant to dispatch it from the Azores in case anything should happen to him on the last leg of the voyage. But he must have changed his mind, because Columbus did not send the letter until he reached the port of Lisbon. Thence the letter traveled by land and its author by sea, but the letter arrived at Barcelona before Columbus did. As a matter of fact, the letter was already printed by the time Columbus entered the city between April 15 and 20.

The letter seems to have been sent to several high-ranking court officials. The one here reprinted is addressed to the treasurer, Gabriel Sánchez. Another copy, from which the first Spanish edition was printed, was addressed to Luis de Santangel. Modern scholarship regards it as a public announcement not addressed to any particular person. News of the Great Discovery traveled very quickly from Spain to Italy. Extracts from Columbus' letter were included in the Papal bull issued on May 3, 1493 which allotted the newly discovered territory to Spain.

Columbus describes eloquently the natural beauties of the New World. Of Hispaniola (Haiti) he relates: "The convenience and superiority of the harbors in this island and its wealth in rivers, joined with wholesomeness for man, is such as to surpass belief unless one has seen them." The fertility of the land and its richness in gold and various metals is emphasized. Columbus seems to be certain that the inhabitants will easily be converted "to the holy faith of Christ" because they are "timid and fearful" and all of them have a common language. The letter was no doubt planned to serve as propaganda for subsequent voyages.

Parallel texts of the four earliest Latin editions of this letter are included in *The Letter of Columbus on the Discovery of America* (New York, 1892), pp. 16-61. An account of the composition of the letter and a critical evaluation of its contents is given in *Admiral of the Ocean Sea* by Samuel Eliot Morison (Boston, 1949), pp. 322-323 and 375-380.

Epistola de Insulis Nuper Inventis

¶ Epistola Christofori Colom: cui etas nostra multū debet: de
Insulis Jndie supra Gangem nuper inuētis.Ad quas pergren/
das octauo antea mense auspiciis τ ere inuictissem:oꝗ Fernādi τ
Delisabet Hispaniaꝗ Regū missus fuerat: ad magnificum dñm
Gabrielem Sanchis eorundē serenissimoꝗ Regum Thesaurariū
missa:quā nobilis ac litteratus vir Leander de Cosco ab Hispa
no idiomate in latinum cōuertit tertio kaƚs Maii· M·cccc·xciii
Pontificatus Alexandri Sexti Anno primo·

Q Uoniam suscepte prouintie rem perfectam me ꝓsecutum
fuisse gratum tibi fore scio:has constitui exarare: que te
vniuscuiusꝗ rei in hoc nostro itinere geste inuenteꝗ ad/
moneant:Tricesimotertio die postꝗ Gadibus discessi in mare
Jndicū perueni:vbi plurimas insulas innumeris habitatas ho/
minibus repperi:quarum omnium pro feliciffimo Rege nostro
preconio celebrato τ vexillis extensis contradicente nemine pos/
seffionem accepi:primeꝗ earum diui Saluatoris nomen impo/
sui:cuius fretus auxilio tam ad hanc:ꝗ ad ceteras alias perue/
nimus·Eam ꝟo Jndi Guanahanin vocant·Aliarū etiam vnam
quanꝗ nouo nomine nuncupaui ; quippe aliā insulam Sancte
Marie Conceptionis·aliam Fernandinam· aliam Hysabellam·
aliam Joanam·τ sic de reliquis appellari iussi·Cum primum in
eam insulam quam dudum Joanam vocari dixi appulimus: iu
xta eius littus occidentem versus aliquantulum procession: tamꝗ
eam magnam nullo ꝛeperto fine inueni:vt non insulā: sed conti
nentem Chatai prouinciam esse crediderim: nulla tñ videns op
pida municipiaue in maritimis sita.confinibꝰ preter aliquos vi/
cos τ prdia rustica:cum quoꝗ incolis loqui nequibam·quare si
mul ac nos videbant surripiebant fugam · Progrediebar vltra
existimans aliquā me vrbem villasue inuenturū·Deniꝗ videns
ꝗ longe admodum progressis nihil noui emergebat:τ hmōi via
nos ad Septentrionem deferebat:ꝗ ipse fugere exoptabā:terris
etenim regnabat bruma:ad Austrumꝗ erat in voto cōtendere:

nec minus venti flagitantib⁹ succedebāt constitui alios nō ope
riri successus: τ sic retrocedens ad portū quendā quem signaue/
ram sum reuersus: vnde duos boies ex noftris in terrā misi: qui
inueitigarēt esset ne Rex in ea prouincia vrbesue aliqueʒ Hi per
tres dies ambularunt inueneruntʒ inumeros populos τ habita/
tiones: paruas tn̄ τ absqʒ vllo regimine · quapropter redierūt·
Interea ego iam intellexeram a qbuſdam Indis quos ibidē ſu/
ſceperā quō bmōi prouincia insula quidem erat: τ sic perrexi ori
entem versus eius ſemp ſtringēs littora vsqʒ ad miliaria·cccxxii
vbi ipsius insule sunt extrema: binc aliā insulam ad oriētē pro
ſperi diſtantē ab bac Joana miliarib⁹·liiii· quā protinus Hiſpa
nam dixi: in eamqʒ conceſſi τ direxi iter quaſi per Septentrionē
quemadmodum in Joana ad orientēʒ miliaria·dlxiiii· que dicta
Joana τ alie ibidē insule ōfertilissime exiſtunt·Hec multis atqʒ
tutiſſimis τ latis nec aliis |quos vnqʒ viderim cōparandis por/
tibus eſt circundata·multi maximi τ ſalubres banc interfluunt
fluuii·multi quoqʒ τ eminentissimi in ea sunt montes·Omnes
be insule sunt pulcherrime τ variis diſtincte figuris: pnie: τ ma/
xima arbor varietate sidera lambentiū plene: quas nunqʒ foliis
priuari credo·Quippe vidi eas ita virentes atqʒ decoras ceu mē
ſe Maio in Hiſpania solent esse: quar alie florētes alie fructuo/
ſe: alie in alio ſtatu ſm vniuſcuiusqʒ qualitatē vigebant: garrie/
bat philomela τ alii passeres varii ac inumeri mēſe Nouembris
quo ipse per eas deambulabā·Sunt preterea in dicta insula Joa
na ſeptē vel octo palmaʒ genera q̄ proceritate τ pulcbritudine
quēadmodū cetere oēs arbores: berbe: fructuſqʒ nr̄as facile exu/
perāt·Sūt τ mirabiles pin⁹ agri τ prata vaſtiſſima: varie aues:
varia mella: variaqʒ metalla ferro excepto·In ea aūt quā Hiſpa
nam ſupra diximꝰ nuncupari maximi sunt mōtes ac pulcbri: va
ſta rura·nemora·campi feraciſſimi ſeri paſciqʒ τ ꝓdendis edifici
is aptiſſimi·portuū in bac insula cōmoditas τ preſtantia flumi
nū copia ſalubritate admixta boimqʒ niſi quis viderit: credulita
rē ſuperat·Huiꝰ arbores paſcua τ fructus multij ab illis Joane

differunt. Hec preterea hispana diuerso aromatis genere. auro
metallisqʒ abundat·cuius quidem ⁊ oĩum aliaꝗ quas ego vidi ⁊
⁊ quaꝗ cognitionẽ habeo incole vtriusqʒ sexus nudi semper ince
dunt quẽadmodũ edunt in lucem:preter aliquas feminas:ꝗ fo
lio frondere aliqua aut bombicino velo pudenda operiunt: qð
ipse sibi ad id negocii parant·Carent ii oẽs (vt supra dixi)quoꝛ
cũqʒ genere ferri·carēt ⁊ armis vtpote sibi ignotis nec ad ea sũt
apti:nõ ꝓpter corporis deformitatem. cũ sint bene formati : sed
qa sunt timidi ac pleni formidine·gestant tñ pro armis arundi
nes sole pustas:in quaꝗ radicibꝰ bastile quoddã ligneũ siccũ et
in mucronem attenuatũ figunt·neqʒ iis audẽt iugiter vti: nã se
pe euenit cũ miserim duos vel tris boies ex meis ad aliquas vil
las vt cũ eaꝗ loquerent incolis:exiisse agmen glomeratũ ex Jn
dis:⁊ vbi nros appropinquare videbant fugã celeriter arripuis
se despretis a patre liberis ⁊ econtra·⁊ hoc nõ ꝗ cuipiam eoꝛ dã
num aliqð vel iniuria illata fuerit:imo ad quoscũqʒ appuli ⁊ qui
bus cũ verbum facere potui:quicqd habebã sum elargitus: pan
num aliaqʒ pmulta nulla mihi facta versura: sed sunt natura pa
uidi ac timidi·Ceteꝛ vbi se cernunt tutos oĩ metu repulso: sunt
admodum simplices ac bone fidei ⁊ in oibꝰ que habẽt liberalissi
mi:roganti qð possidet inficiat nemo:quin ipsi nos ad id posce
dũ inuitãt·Maximũ erga oẽs amorẽ preseferunt:dant queqʒ ma
gna pro paruis:minima lʒ re nihiloue ꝛtenti·ego attñ phibui ne
tã minia ⁊ nulliꝰ precii bisce darent : vt sunt lancis· parapsidu·
vitriqʒ fragmenta·itẽ claui ligule·quãqʒ si hoc poterãt adipisci
videbat eis pulcherrima mũdi possidere iocalia·Accidit·n· que
dam nauitam tantũ auri põdus habuisse pro vna ligula quantj
sunt tres aurei solidi·⁊ sic alios pro aliis minoris precii:psertim
pro blanquis nouis:quibusdã nũmis aureis: ꝑ qbꝰ habẽdis da
bant quicquid petebat vẽditor: puta vnciam cũ dimidia ⁊ duas
auri:vel triginta ⁊ quadraginta bombicis pondo: quã ipsi iam
nouerant·itẽ arcuum·amphore·hydrie·doliiqʒ fragmenta bom
bice ⁊ auro tanqʒ bestie comparabant·quod quia iniquum sane

erat vetui: dedi$q$ eis multa pulchra τ grata q̄ mecū : ulerā nul
lo interueniente premio vt eos mihi facilius xiliarem fieren$q$
xpicole τ vt sint proni in amorem erga Regē Reginā principēq
nostros τ vniuersas gentes Dispanie ac studeant perquirere co
aceruare eac$q$ nobis tradere quib? ipsi affluunt τ nos magnope
re indigemus. Aullam ii norunt idolatriam: imo firmissime cre
dūt oēm vim: oēm potentiam: oīa deni$q$ bona esse in celo : me$q$
inde cum his nauibus τ nautis descēdisse: at$q$ hoc animo vbi$q$
fui susceptus post$q$ metum repulerant. Aec sunt segnes aut ru
des: quin summi ac perspicacis ingenii: τ homines qui transfre
tant mare illud nō sine admiratiōe vniuscuius$q$ rei ratiōe red
dunt: sed nun$q$ viderūt gentes restitas neq$ naues hmōi. Ego
statim at$q$ ad mare illud perueni e prima insula quosdā Jndos
violenter arripui: qui ediscerent a nobis τ nos pariter docerent
eā quo$q$ ipsi in iisce partibus cognitionem habebant : τ ex voto
successit: nam breui nos ipsos: τ ii nos tum gestu ac signis: tum
verbis intellexerunt: magno$q$ nobis fure emolumento: reniūt
modo mecum qui semper putant me desiluisse e celo: quāuis diu
nobiscum versati fuerint hodie$q$ versentur: et ii erant primi qui
id quocun$q$ appellabamus nuntiabant: alii deinceps aliis ela
ta voce dicentes: Uenite venite τ videbitis gētes ethereas Quā
ob rem tam femine q viri: tam impuberes q adulti : tā iuuenes
q senes deposita formidine paulo ante ꝫcepta nos certatim vise
bant magna iter stipante caterua: aliis cibum: aliis potum affe
rentibus maximo cum amore ac beniuolentia incredibili. Dabet
vnaque$q$ insula multas scaphas solidi ligni: τ si angustas lon
gitudine tn ac forma nostris biremibus similes: cursu aūt velo
ciores. Reguntur remis tantūmodo. Daq quedaz sunt magne:
quedam parue: quedā in medio consistūt. Plures tn biremi que
remiget duodeuiginti transtris maiores: cū quibus in oēs illas
insulas: que innumere sunt: traiicitur. cumq$ iis suam mercatu
ram exercent τ inter eos comertia fiunt. Aliquas ego harum bi
remiū seu scaphaz vidi q̄ vehebant septuaginta τ octuaginta re

rii ges. In omnibus iterum insulis nulla est diuersitas inter gentis
effigies: nulla in moribus atq loquela: quin oes se intelligunt
adinuicem: que res perutilis est ad id qd serenissimos Reges no
stros exoptare precipue reor: scz eoy ad sctam rpi fidem puersio
nem: cui qdem quantu intelligere potui facillimi sunt et proni.
Dixi quemadmodu sum progressus antea insulam Joanam per re
ctam tramitem occasus in orientem miliaria ccccxxii. s m qua via
z interuallum itineris possum dicere banc Joanam esse maiore
Anglia z Scotia simul: nacq vltra dicta ccccxxii passuu milia in
ea parte que ad occidentem prospectat due: quas no petii: super
sunt prouincie quay altera Jndi Anan vocant cuius accole cau
dati nascuntur. Tendunt in longitudinez ad miliaria. clxxx. vt
ab his quos vebo mecu Jndis percepi: qui ois bas callent insu
las. Hispane bo ambit? maior est tota Hispania a Colonia vsq
ad fontem rabidum. Hincq facile arguit q quartum eius latus
quod ipse per recta linea occidentis in orientem traieci miliaria
continet dxl. Hec insula est affectanda z affectata no spernenda
In qua z si aliay oim vt dixi pro inuictissimo Rege nostro sclen
niter possessionem accepi: earuq imperium dicto Regi penitus
comittitur: in oportuniori tn loco atq cmni lucro et ccmertio
condecenti cuiusda magne ville: cui Natiuitatis dni nomen de
dimus: possessionem peculiariter accepi: ibiq arcem quanda
erigere extemplo iussi: que modo iam debet esse pacta: in qua ho
mines qui necessarii sunt visi cu cmni ai moy genere z vltra an
num victu oportuno reliqui. Item quanda carauella z pro aliis
construendis tam in bac arte q in ceteris peritos: ac eiusde in
sule Regis erga eos beniuolentiam z familiaritate incredibile
Sunt enim gentes ille amabiles admodum z benigne: eo q Rex
predictus me fratre suu dici gloriabat. Et si aium reuocarent et
iis qui in arce manserunt nocere velint: nequeunt: qa armis ca
rent: nudi incedunt z nimiu timidi: ideo dicta arcem tenetes dun
taxat pnt tota eam insulam nullo sibi iminete discrimine popu
lari: dummo leges quas dedim? ac regimen no excedat. Jn oiba

iis insulis vt intellexi quisq̃ vni tm̃ ꝑiugi acquiescit:pꝛeter pꝛin
cipes aut reges:qbus viginti hie licet·Femine magis q̃ viri la
boꝛare videntur·nec bene potui intelligere an habeãt bona pꝛo
pꝛia:vidi enim ꝙ vnus habebat aliis impartiri:pꝛesertim dapes
obsonia ꝉ hm̃oĩ·Nullum apud eos monstrũ reperi vt pleriq̃ exi
stimabant:sed hoies magne reuerentie atꝗ benignos· Hec sunt
nigri velut ethiopes·habent crines planos ꝉ demissos· non de
gũt vbi radioꝛ solaris emicat caloꝛ·pmagna nanꝗ hic est solis
vehementia:pꝛopterea ꝙ ab equinoctiali linea distat·Ubi vide
tur gradus sex ꝉ viginti ex montiũ cacuminib?·Maximũ quoꝗ
viget frigus:sed id qdem moderantur Jndi tum loci cõsuetudi
ne·tum rerũ calidissimaꝛ quib? frequenter ꝉ luxuriose vescunt
pꝛesidio· Jtaꝗ mõstra aliqua nõ vidi:neꝗ eoꝛ alicubi habui co
gnitionem:excepta quadã insula Charis nuncupata: que secun
da ex Hispania in Jndiam transfretantib? existit·quã gens que
dam a finitimis habita ferocioꝛ incolit·Hi carne humana vescũ
tur·Habent pꝛedicti biremiũ genera plurima qbus in ois Jndi
cas insulas traiiciunt·depꝛedant·surripiunt quecũꝗ pñt· Nihil
ab aliis differunt nisi ꝙ gerũt moꝛe femineo longos crines·rtũ
tur arcub? ꝉ spiculis arundineis fixis vt diximᵘ in grossioꝛi par
te attenuatis hastilib?·ideoꝗ habent̃ feroces:quare ceteri Jndi
inexhausto metu plectunt:sed hos ego nihili facio plus q̃ alios
Hi sunt q cobeunt cũ quibusdã feminis:que sole insulã Mateu
nin pꝛimã ex Hispania in Jndiã traiicientib? habitant· De aũt
femine nullũ sui sexus opus exercent:vtuntur enim arcubus et
spiculis sicut de eaꝛ ꝑiugibus dixi·muniunt sese laminis eneis
quaꝛ maxima apud eas copia existit·Aliã mihi insulã affirmãt
supꝛadicta Hispana maioꝛe:eius incole carẽt pilis· auroꝗ inter
alias potissimũ exuberat·Huius insule ꝉ aliaꝛ quas vidi hoies
mecũ poꝛto qui hoꝛ que dixi testimoniũ perhibẽt·Deniꝗ vt nõ
stri discessus ꝉ celeris reuersionis compendiũ ac emolumentum
bꝛeuibus astringã hoc polliceoꝛ:me nostris Regibus inuictissi
mis paruo eoꝛ fultũ auxilio:tantũ auri daturũ quantũ eis fue

rſt opus.tm̄ vero aromatum.bombicis.maſticis:q̄ apud Cbium
diuraxat innenitur. tantūq̄ ligni aloes. tantum ſeruoꝗ bydo/
latrarum :quantum eoꝛum maieſtas voluerit erigere. item reu/
barbarum ꞇ alia aromatum genera que ii quos in dicta arce reli
qui ſam inueniſſe atꝗ inuenturos exiſtimo · q̄nquidem ego nul
libi magis ſum moꝛatus niſī quantum me coegerunt venti:pꝛe/
terꝗ in villa Aatiuitatis:dum arcez condere ꞇ tuta oīa eſſe pꝛo
uidi.Que ꞇ ſi maxima ꞇ inaudita ſunt:multo tn̄ maioꝛa foꝛent
ſi naues mibi vt ratio exigit ſubueniſſent.Ueꝗ mul:um ac mira
bile boc:nec noſtris meritis coꝛreſpondens:ſed ſancte Cbꝛiſtia/
ne fidei:noſtroꝛumꝗ Regum pietati ac religioni: quia quod bu
manus conſequi nō poterat intellectus:id bu̇manis cōceſſit di
uinus·Solet enim deus ſeruꝰs ſuos:quiꝗ ſua pꝛecepta diligūt
ꞇ in impoſſibilibus exaudire:vt nobis in pꝛeſentia contigit:qui
ea conſecuti ſumus que bactenus moꝛtalium vires minime atti
gerant:nam ſi barū inſulaꝗ quipiam aliquid ſcripſerunt aut lo
cuti ſunt:omnes per ambages ꞇ cōiecturas·nemo ſe eas vidiſſe
aſſerit vnde pꝛop: vi lebatur fabula·Igitur Rex ꞇ Regina pꝛin
cepſꝗ ac eoꝗ regna feli:iſſ ma cunctecꝗ ali: Cbꝛiſtianoꝗ pꝛouin
cie Saluatoꝛi dn̄o noſtro Jeſu Cbꝛiſto agam? gratias: qui tan
ta nos victo:ia munerecꝗ donauit:celebꝛentur pꝛoceſſiones·per
agantur ſolennia ſacra:feſtaꝗ fronde velentur delubꝛa· exultet
Cbꝛiſtus in terris quemadmodum in celis exultat:quom tot po
puloꝛum perditas ante bac animas ſaluatum iri pꝛeuidet·Lete
mur ꞇ nos:cum pꝛopter exaltationem noſtre fidei· tum pꝛopter
rerum tempoꝛalium incrementa:quoꝗ non ſolum Hiſpania ſed
vniuerſa Cbꝛiſtianitas eſt futura particeps· Hec vt geſta ſunt
ſic bꝛeuiter enarrata.Uale·Uliſbone pꝛidie Jdus Martii·

Cbꝛiſtofoꝛus Colom Oceane claſſis Pꝛefectus·

¶ Epigramma·R·L·de Corbaria Episcopi Montispalusii
Ad Inuictissimum Regem Hispaniarum.

Iam nulla Hispanis tellus addenda Triumphis
  Atqz parum tantis viribus orbis erat·
Nunc longe Eois regio deprensa sub vndis·
  Auctura est titulos Betice magne tuos:
Vnde repertori merito referenda Colombo
  Gratia: sed summo est maior habenda deo·
Qui vincenda parat noua Regna tibiqz sibiqz
  Teqz simul fortem prestat z esse pium·

The Columbus Letter of 1493
A New Translation in English
by Frank E. Robbins

THE letter of Christopher Columbus, to whom our age owes a great debt, on the recent discovery of the islands of India beyond the Ganges, to look for which he had been sent eight months before under the auspices and at the expense of the most invincible Ferdinand and Isabella, sovereigns of the Spains; sent to the eminent lord Gabriel Sánchez, treasurer of the said most serene sovereigns; which the noble and learned gentleman, Leander di Cosco, translated from Spanish into Latin the third day before the Kalends of May,[1] 1493, in the first year of the pontificate of Alexander VI.

1. *April 29.*

A S I know that it will please you that I have carried to completion the duty which I assumed, I decided to write you this letter to advise you of every single event and discovery of this voyage of ours. On the thirty-third day after I left Cadiz;[1] I reached the Indian Sea, there I found very many islands, inhabited by numberless people, of all of which I took possession without opposition in the name of our most fortunate king by making formal proclamation and raising standards; and to the first of them I gave the name of San Salvador,[2] the blessed Savior, through dependence on whose aid we reached both this and the others. The Indians however call it Guanahani. I gave each one of the others too a new name; to wit, one Santa Maria de la Concepción,[3] another Fernandina,[4] another Isabella,[5] another Juana,[6] and I ordered similar names to be used for the rest.

When we first put in at the island which I have just said was named Juana, I proceeded along its shore westward a little way, and found it so large (for no end to it appeared) that I believed it to be no island but the continental province of Cathay; without seeing, however, any towns or cities situated in its coastal parts except a few villages and rustic farms, with whose inhabitants I could not talk because they took to flight as soon as they saw us.

I went on further, thinking that I would find a city or some farmhouses. Finally, seeing that nothing new turned

1. *Translator's error for "the Canaries," where Columbus put in on his westward voyage. He did not touch at Cadiz at all.*

2. *Watling's Island in the Bahamas.*

3. *Rum Cay.*

4. *Long Island.*

5. *Crooked Island.*

6. *Cuba. Columbus called it Juana in honor of the Infant Don Juan.*

[8]

up, though we had gone far enough, and that this course was carrying us off to the north (a thing which I myself wanted to avoid, for winter prevailed on those lands, and it was my hope to hasten to the south) and since the winds too were favorable to our desires, I concluded that no other means of accomplishment offered, and thus reversing my course I returned to a certain harbor which I had marked and from that point sent ashore two men of our number to find out whether there was a king in that province, or any cities. These men proceeded afoot for three days and found countless people and inhabited places, but all small and without any government; and therefore they returned.

In the meantime I had already learned from some Indians whom I had taken aboard at this same place that this province was in fact an island; and so I went on toward the east, always skirting close to its shores, for 322 miles, where is the extremity of the island. From this point I observed another island to eastward, 54 miles from this island Juana, which I immediately called Hispana.[1] I withdrew to it, and set my course along its northern coast, as I had at Juana, to the east for 564 miles.

The before-mentioned island Juana and the other islands of the region, too, are as fertile as they can be. This one is surrounded by harbors, numerous, very safe and broad, and not to be compared with any others that I have seen anywhere; many large, wholesome rivers flow through this land; and there are also many very lofty mountains in it. All these islands are most beautiful and distinguished by various forms; one can travel through them, and they are full of trees of the greatest variety,

1. *Hispaniola (San Domingo or Haiti). Columbus greatly overestimated the dimensions of these islands.*

[9]

which brush at the stars; and I believe they never lose their foliage. At any rate, I found them as green and beautiful as they usually are in the month of May in Spain; some of them were in bloom, some loaded with fruit, some flourished in one state, others in the other, each according to its kind; the nightingale was singing and there were countless other birds of many kinds in the month of November when I myself was making my way through them. There are furthermore, in the before-mentioned island Juana, seven or eight kinds of palm trees, which easily surpass ours in height and beauty, as do all the other trees, grasses, and fruits. There are also remarkable pines, vast fields and meadows, many kinds of birds, many kinds of honey, and many kinds of metals, except iron.

There are moreover in that island which I said above was called Hispaniola fine, high mountains, broad stretches of country, forests, and extremely fruitful fields excellently adapted for sowing, grazing, and building dwelling houses. The convenience and superiority of the harbors in this island and its wealth in rivers, joined with wholesomeness for man, is such as to surpass belief unless one has seen them. The trees, coverage, and fruits of this island are very different from those of Juana. Besides, this Hispaniola is rich in various kinds of spice and in gold and in mines, and its inhabitants (and those of all the others which I saw, and of which I have knowledge) of either sex always go as naked as when they were born, except some women who cover their private parts with a leaf or a branch of some sort, or with a skirt of cotton which they themselves prepare for the purpose.

They all of them lack, as I said above, iron of whatever kind, as well as arms, for these are unknown to them; nor are they fitted for weapons, not because of any bodily deformity, for they are well built, but in that they are timid and fearful. However, instead of arms they carry reeds baked in the sun, in the roots of which they fasten a sort of spearhead made of dry wood and sharpened to a point. And they do not dare to use these at close quarters; for it often happened that when I had sent two or three of my men to certain farmhouses to talk with their inhabitants a closely packed body of Indians would come out and when they saw our men approach they would quickly take flight, children deserted by father and vice versa; and that too not that any hurt or injury had been brought upon a single one of them; on the contrary, whenever I approached any of them and whenever I could talk with any of them I was generous in giving them whatever I had, cloth and very many other things, without any return being made to me; but they are naturally fearful and timid.

However when they see that they are safe and all fear has been dispelled they are exceedingly straightforward and trustworthy and most liberal with all that they have; none of them denies to the asker anything that he possesses; on the contrary they themselves invite us to ask for it. They exhibit great affection to all and always give much for little, content with very little or nothing in return. However I forbade such insignificant and valueless things to be given to them, as pieces of platters, dishes, and glass, or again nails and lace points;[1] though if they could acquire such it seemed to them that they possessed the most beautiful trinkets in the world. For it happened that one sailor got in return for one lace point a weight of gold equivalent to three golden solidi,[2] and similarly others in

1. *The tips of the laces used to secure the hose to the upper garment.*
2. Castellanos *in the Spanish version.*

exchange for other things of slighter value; especially in exchange for brand-new blancas, certain gold coins, to secure which they would give whatever the seller asks, for example, an ounce and a half or two ounces of gold, or thirty or forty [pounds] of cotton by weight, which they themselves had spun;[1] likewise they bought pieces of hoops,[2] pots, pitchers, and jars for cotton and gold, like dumb beasts. I forbade this, because it was clearly unjust, and gave them free many pretty and acceptable objects that I had brought with me, in order more easily to win them over to me, and that they might become Christians, and be inclined to love our King and Queen and Prince and all the peoples of Spain, and to make them diligent to seek out and accumulate and exchange with us the articles in which they abound and which we greatly need.

They know nothing of idolatry; on the contrary they confidently believe that all might, all power, all good things, in fact, are in the heavens; they thought that I too had descended thence with these ships and sailors, and in that opinion I was received everywhere after they had rid themselves of fear. Nor are they slow or ignorant; on the contrary, they are of the highest and keenest wit; and the men who navigate that sea give an admirable account of each detail; but they have never seen men wearing clothes, or ships of this sort. As soon as I came to that sea I forcibly seized some Indians from the first island, so that they might learn from us and similarly teach us the things of which they had knowledge in those parts; and it came out just as I had hoped; for we quickly taught them, and

1. Nouerant, *"had known,"* which stands in the text, is a mistake for neuerant, *"had spun."*

2. *The Spanish text has here* "hoops of winecasks," *which Leander probably intends by the word* arcuum, *"bows."*

[12]

then they us, by gestures and signs; finally they understood by means of words, and it paid us well to have them.
The ones who now go with me persist in the belief that I
leaped down out of the skies, although they have associ-
ated with us for a long time and are still doing so today;
and they were the first to announce that fact wherever
we landed, some of them calling out loudly to the others,
"Come, come, and you will see the men from heaven."
And so women as well as men, children and grown people,
youths and old men, laying aside the fear they had con-
ceived shortly before, vied with each other in coming to
look at us, the great crowd of them clogging the road,
some bringing food, others drink, with the greatest mani-
festation of affection and unbelievable good will.

Each island possesses many canoes of solid wood, and
though they are narrow, nevertheless in length and shape
they are like our double-banked galleys, but faster. They
are steered with oars alone. Some of these are large, some
small, some of medium size; a considerable number however are larger than the galley which is rowed by eighteen
benches. With these they cross to all the islands, which
are innumerable, and with them they ply their trade, and
commerce is carried out between them. I saw some of
these galleys or canoes which carried seventy or eighty
oarsmen.

In all the islands there is no difference in the appearance
of the people, nor in their habits or language; on the contrary, they all understand each other, which circumstance
is most useful to that end which I think our most serene
sovereigns especially desire, namely, their conversion to
the holy faith of Christ, to which indeed as far as I could
see they are readily submissive and inclined.

I have told how I sailed along the island of Juana on a

straight course from west to east 322 miles; from this voyage and the length of the course I can say that this Juana is larger than England and Scotland together; for beyond the aforesaid 322 miles, in the western part, there are two more provinces which I did not visit, one of which the Indians call Anan, whose inhabitants are born with tails. These provinces extend to a length of 180 miles, as I have found out from these Indians whom I am bringing with me, who are well acquainted with all these islands.

The circumference of Hispaniola, indeed, is more than all Spain from Catalonia to Fuenterrabia. And this is easily proved by this fact, that the one of its four sides which I myself traversed on a straight course from west to east measures 540 miles. We should seek possession of this island and once gained it is not to be thrown away; for although, as I said, I formally took possession of all the others in the name of our invincible King and their sovereignty is entirely committed to that said King, nevertheless in this island I took possession in a special way of a certain large village in a more favorable situation, suitable for all sorts of gain and trade, to which I gave the name Navidad del Señor; and I gave orders to erect a fort there at once. This should by now be built, and in it I left behind the men who seemed necessary with all kinds of arms and suitable food for more than a year, furthermore, one caravel,[1] and for the construction of others men skilled in this art as well as in others; and, besides, an unbelievable goodwill and friendship on the part of the king of that island toward the men. For all those peoples are so gentle and kind that the aforesaid king took pride in my being called his brother. Even if they should change their minds and want to injure the men who stayed in the fort they cannot,

1. The Santa Maria, which was wrecked off this coast.

since they have no arms, go naked, and are extremely timid; and so if our men only hold the said fort they can hold
the whole island, with no hazard on the part of the people
to threaten them as long as they do not depart from the
laws and government which I gave them.[1]

In all those islands, as I understood it, each man is content with only one wife, except the princes or kings, who
may have twenty. The women seem to do more work than
the men. I could not clearly make out whether they have
private property, for I noted that what an individual had
he shared with others, especially food, meats, and the like.
I did not find any monsters among them, as many expect-
ed, but men of great dignity and kindliness. Nor are they
black, like the Negroes; they have long, straight hair; they
do not live where the heat of the sun's rays shines forth;
for the strength of the sun is very great here, since appar-
ently it is only twenty-six degrees from the equator.[2] On
the mountain peaks extreme cold reigns, but this the Indians mitigate both by being used to the region and by the
aid of very hot foods upon which they dine often and
luxuriously.

And so I did not see any monsters, nor do I have knowledge of them anywhere with the exception of a certain island called Charis,[3] which is the second as you sail from
Spain toward India and which a tribe inhabits that is held
by its neighbors to be extremely savage. These feed on
human flesh. The aforesaid have many kinds of galleys in

1. *But the Spaniards did not behave themselves and the whole colony was de-
stroyed before Columbus returned to it on his Second Voyage.*

2. *The text is corrupt and the translation follows the obvious sense. Probably*
ubi videntur *is a mistake for* ut videtur; *the punctuation is wrong, too.*

3. *Probably Puerto Rico. The name Charis is derived from that of the savage
tribe here mentioned, the Caribs, who were much feared by the Tainos found
by Columbus in the Bahamas, Cuba, and Hispaniola.*

which they cross to all the Indian islands, rob, and steal all they can. They differ in no respect from the others, except that in feminine fashion they wear their hair long; and they use bows and arrows with shafts of reeds fitted as we said at the thicker end with sharpened arrowheads. On that account they are held to be savage, and the other Indians are afflicted with constant fear of them, but I do not rate them any more highly than the rest. These are the ones who cohabit with certain women who are the only inhabitants of the island of Mateunin,[1] which is the first encountered in the passage from Spain toward India. These women moreover, do not occupy themselves with any of the work that properly belongs to their sex, for they use bows and arrows just as I related of their husbands; they protect themselves with copper plates of which there is an ample supply in their land. They assure me that there is another island larger than the abovementioned Hispaniola; its inhabitants are hairless, and it abounds in gold more than all the others. I am bringing with me men from this island and the others that I saw who bear testimony to what I have said.

Finally, to compress into a few words the advantage and profit of our journey hence and our speedy return, I make this promise, that supported by only small aid from them I will give our invincible sovereigns as much gold as they need, as much spices, cotton, and the mastic, which is found only in Chios,[2] as much of the wood of the aloe, as many slaves to serve as sailors as their Majesties wish to

1. *Martinique. Columbus was prepared to find an island inhabited by men and another inhabited by women in the Indian Ocean (where he thought he was), because he had read about them in his copy of Marco Polo's travels.*

2. *Columbus probably visited Chios in a Genoese trading ship in 1474 and 1475 (Morison,* Admiral of the Ocean Sea, *I, 31).*

demand; furthermore, rhubarb and other kinds of spices which I suppose those whom I left in the before-mentioned fort have already discovered and will discover, since indeed I lingered nowhere longer than the winds compelled, except at the village of Navidad while I took care to establish the fort and to make all safe. Though these things are great and unheard of, nevertheless they would have been much greater if the ships had served me as they reasonably should.[1]

Indeed this outcome was manifold and marvelous, and fitting not to my own claims to merit, but rather to the holy Christian faith and the piety and religion of our sovereigns, for what the human mind could not comprehend, that the divine mind has granted to men. For God is accustomed to listen to his servants, and to those who love his commands, even in impossible circumstances, as has happened to us in the present instance, for we have succeeded in that to which hitherto mortal powers have in no wise attained. For if others have written or spoken of these islands, they have all done so by indirection and guesses; no one claims to have seen them, whence it seemed to be almost a fable. Therefore let the King and Queen, the Prince, their happy realms, and all other provinces of Christendom give thanks to the Savior, our Lord Jesus Christ, who has granted us so great a victory and reward; let processions be celebrated; let solemn holy rites be

1. *This may refer to the conduct of Martín Alonso Pinzón and to the carelessness that permitted* Santa Maria *to run aground. Pinzón, never too cooperative, took* Pinta *on an exploring and gold-hunting trip (November 22, 1492-January 6, 1493) without the Admiral's permission. Columbus made* Santa Maria *his flagship, but Juan de la Cosa was her master and part owner, and officer of the watch at the time of the disaster. He seems to have been not only negligent but also cowardly and insubordinate (see Morison, op. cit., I, 388-389).*

performed; and let the churches be decked with festival branches; let Christ rejoice on earth as He does in heaven when He foresees that so many souls of peoples hitherto lost are to be saved. Let us too rejoice, both for the exaltation of our faith and for the increase in temporal goods in which not only Spain but all Christendom together are to share. As these things were done, so have they been briefly narrated. Farewell.

Lisbon, the day before the Ides of March.[1]

CHRISTOPHER COLUMBUS
Admiral of the Ocean Fleet

Epigram of R. L. de Corbaria, Bishop of Monte Peloso; to the most invincible King of Spain.

Lately was there no more land to be added to the triumphs of Spain, and the world was too small for such powers; now a realm discovered afar under the Eastern waves is to increase thy titles, great Baetic; wherefore properly must we give thanks to Columbus, the finder, but greater thanks to all highest God, who provides new realms for thee and for himself, and who warrants thee to be at once mighty and pious.

1. *March* 14.

DATE